FINDING THE FUNNY FAST!

*How to create quick humor to connect
with clients, coworkers and crowds*

By Jan McInnis

Cover design by Steve Dickenson
Book Design & Back Cover by Nikki Ward, Morrison Alley Design

First Printing 2009

ISBN 978-0-9840999-0-0

To my family, the people I like to laugh with the most:
Mom, Dad, Debbie, Tad, Dan, Robin, Brenda,
Glenn, Kathy, Frank, Christine and all my nieces and
nephews who give me a lot of my comedy material!

TABLE OF CONTENTS

INTRODUCTION

Don't wait for permission from others to use humor.
Anyone *can add humor to their communications.*

Thanks for picking up this book and having an interest in being funny or funnier. Regardless of how you communicate or with whom you communicate, there's usually room for some laughs. I don't think people use enough humor. Maybe no one's ever said you're funny, so you think you must not be. Maybe you think it will take hours and hours to craft the perfect line, and, well, who has time for that? Or maybe you're simply afraid the joke you craft might bomb. So you take the safe route. Unfortunately the safe route makes for a boring or ineffective sales letter, memo or speech. What a waste! We humans may be the only species that has the ability to poke fun through language, yet we underuse this ability. Wikipedia, the online dictionary, says that pretty much every organism communicates. Even fungus communicates. (I'm thinking, what does fungus say? *"Hey, Jan just cleaned her bathroom. Let's multiply!"*) But fungus can't make jokes. We can, but we pass up opportunity after opportunity.

NOTE

Sometimes we're funny when we don't mean to be. My mom had a great sense of humor. One time we were watching one of those 3-D movies in which you wear those glasses and the stuff pops off the screen at you. Five minutes in, mom leans over and says "Jan, this stuff is coming right at me, switch seats with me!"

Well, it's time to stop missing out on the fun and start enjoying your communications. Using humor is even more crucial now when we hear so much bad news about the economy. So why not stand out from the doom and gloom and find some lighter ways to communicate?

I wrote this short book about writing humor fast because, aside from the fact that I don't have patience, that's how I write—fast. I got into comedy late in the game (I was almost 34 years old!) so I didn't have years to craft jokes. I had to write fast and get my act on the road quick. And then I started selling material, and it really benefitted me to write fast. Why spend eight hours writing 15 jokes every day for radio when I could do it in two hours and move on to other projects? I was also able to connect with corporate and association clients by writing fast jokes about their businesses and including them in my act. Finding the funny fast is a habit I've developed, and you can, too. So let's do it more!

Can You Really Do This?

Most people think that you're either born to be funny or you have to have some sort of comic "gift." "Oh, I'm not funny like you. I could never do that," is the common line people give me for not even trying to spice up their communications with some laughs. But humor is not something that only a select few people can do. I was a marketing director for 15 years before becoming a comedian. Nobody really ever encouraged me to quit my day job and go into comedy, and I was never the class clown—the one constantly cracking all of those jokes back in school. And trust me, nobody ever came up to me and told me I could write a joke. OK, wait. I take that back. One person in high school saw my raw talent! The only person on the planet who ever told me I was funny was my friend Judy. Back during senior year in high school, we had to vote on those superlatives, you know, like the person who is "Best Dressed," or "Most Athletic" or "I'm Better Than You"—those labels that make the rest of us realize we're bland and not popular. Well, Judy, who I'd known since kindergarten, came up to me one day and said, "Jan, you've always been making kind of funny comments on the side, so I'm going to vote for you as Funniest." That meant I got two votes—mine and Judy's.

Fast forward 30 years later to our class reunion and she's the only one who, when I told her I was a comedian, said without hesitating, "That is perfect for you! What a great job." Everybody else looked at me like they were about to blurt out, "Oh, you're a comedian? Are still living with your parents?" Even a couple of brave souls commented, "I don't recall your being funny." Oh well.

So I didn't get a lot of encouragement to use humor, and I didn't wait for permission to try humor. I became a comedian because I wanted to—it seemed like a fun career. I started writing material for myself and for other people fast because I needed to—I needed money, I needed writing credits and I needed to build my act.

Why Listen to My Advice on Humor Writing?

All the humor writing tips in this book are distilled from my own experiences and research. And by research I mean I wrote jokes, got on stage millions of times and did my best to be funny. And after much trial and error, along with watching other successful comics, I figured it out. I've made a great living telling and selling comedy material for the past 16-plus years. I've seen and done all the right and wrong things in using humor, which means I know how to help you write and speak funnier, too.

Customized Humor

Not all the jokes I write go into my act permanently. I write lots of material for the groups that I perform for. I've been in front of all types of corporations, associations and

> ## *NOTE*
>
> *Topical jokes are a way to write fast humor that's fresh, and I've sold thousands of them. Just a few examples:*
>
> *"CNN reports that this Superbowl weekend lots of vendors will be selling counterfeit sports items that aren't officially licensed by the NFL. An NFL spokesperson said that you can tell if the T-shirt is not an official Super Bowl T-shirt if you can afford it."*
>
> *"A new experimental drug for lowering blood pressure is close to FDA approval. Scientists say it will be almost as effective as a good divorce."*
>
> *"Beware at your cookouts this summer. Bug zappers kill flies and spread their germs up to six feet, which means they can contaminate food on your grill. In fact, you can tell if your hamburgers are getting insect germs—if they taste like hot dogs."*
>
> *"Disneyland has lightened its security procedures. Now if you're caught shoplifting, you have to go to jail for five years. That's much shorter than the previous sentence of standing in line at Space Mountain."*

businesses, including hundreds of esoteric groups (the Mushroom Institute and the Alfalfa Seed Growers come to mind), and I almost always write industry-specific material for them. I started writing customized material by accident. When I was still working comedy clubs, I decided I wanted to get into the convention circuit; it was a bit more lucrative and they seemed more my kind of crowds. But I was a little short of material that was appropriate for these business crowds. I didn't rely on dirty jokes, but some of my act wasn't right for these events. And, as I already mentioned, I'm impatient, so I went ahead and booked convention work anyway, and figured I'd just write customized jokes for each group. It worked!

And, in fact, I still do customized humor today because I found out that not only am I good at it, but that I *enjoy* writing about the different groups. It makes my act fresh to me (Hey, I've heard my jokes!) and usually the client loves that I've included them in the show. It's also a great way to connect right off the bat with an audience. When you can joke about a group, you become one of them, and they will (usually) listen to the rest of what you have to say.

Now I've even expanded my customization to include sitting in on their conference sessions and writing jokes about what they learned that day. Then I jump on stage and recap it all with a "what we just learned" approach. I write 20 or 30 jokes for each group, which can be about 10 minutes of new, not-really-tested material right up front.

Writing for CEOs and Other Non-Professional Speakers

As I got good at writing for my shows, I expanded into writing for other people who may speak professionally or do a lot of writing in their jobs but whose focus is something else. This includes selling material to CEOs who want to put some fun into their communications. They realize that people don't want to hear a boring speech about the company goals or the foundation's activities unless there's something in it for them. And if the employees aren't getting a dividend check, then the "something in it for them" should at least be an entertaining speech. I've also written for doctors and other professionals who have to speak or emcee at an event and don't really have time to come up with funny stuff.

Other Professional Speakers

A lot of professional speakers are great subject matter experts, but they don't have time to punch up an entire 60-minute keynote. Even if they bought this book, they'd rather spend their time drumming up business and honing their expertise, while letting me do the comedy writing. That's great with me! I'm a quick study and I pride myself on being able to figure out their business and then punch out great, on-target material fast.

Radio

A lot of morning DJs come in at 4:30 a.m. and they don't have time to find news stories or weird stories, so they subscribe to a radio prep service. The service sends 40 or 50 pages of wacky news and showbiz sex stories, plus jokes and top 10 lists, so when the DJs hit the air at 5 a.m., they have material and can jump right into the show. I wrote for a radio prep service for 10 years. It's really fast writing because they wanted 15 topical jokes a day. Even if I didn't sell all 15 jokes, I did pretty well— and I punched them out in about two hours. Of course, many DJs write their own funny stuff, but the prep services are a nice addition. Britney Spears's drunken antics have paid my mortgage for years.

TV Shows

I've freelanced material for several TV shows, most notably *The Tonight Show*. I was never a staff writer on the show, but I sold some jokes and had some fun with it. It was good for my ego to get some jokes on there. One night I was coming back from some comedy clubs in LA where every comic on the planet but me, it seemed, had some sort of "deal" they were working on. I was feeling kind of low until I flipped on the TV and there was Leno doing a joke I'd submitted that day. Cool!

Greeting Cards

I've written for greeting cards, which is very hard. They have to be specific, yet general. A Mother's Day card has to appeal to a mother who is young, who is old, who has kids at home, who has grown kids. You get the picture. They pay the best, but good, specific-general material is harder to come up with.

So the moral of this story is, I've written a lot of humor for every type of venue, so I can give you the scoop on how to do it, too. Perhaps you just want to quickly add some humor to a speech because you've got to follow Bill Gates. Or maybe you have to send out a sales letter on a dry topic and you want people to actually read it. Or maybe you're in the medical profession and you want to cheer up your patients' hospital experiences. Whatever your reasons for adding more fun stuff to your communications, I'm happy to help.

NOTE

I've written for lots of people, including CEOs, speakers and doctors emceeing events. Here are some examples for a jewelry auction:

"We have a lot more doctors in the room than in past years. Word must have gotten out about how violent the silent auction can get."

"We'll be starting the bidding for the high-end live auction items as soon as my wife leaves to use the restroom. TAG: I'm trying to time it this year to save myself some money."

"I love our hospital community. We have a great mix of people—some who are financially secure and some who are broke. And some of us changed categories just this evening after our wives bought jewelry."

1

WHY PUT HUMOR IN YOUR COMMUNICATIONS?

I used to do "joke of the day" at my lunch table in junior high school. It got us in the mood to eat cafeteria food!

You picked up this book because you have a specific reason for adding humor to your speeches, sales pitches, or memos—or as one woman at my humor-writing seminar said, "Because the other seminars were full." Of course, she said that *after* I taught her how to write jokes, so I'm guessing she was joking. But there are lots of benefits to including humor. Here's the short list.

Humor Makes Your Message Memorable.

If you want your point to be remembered, make it funny. I sit in on lots of conference sessions and then kick off my program with some funny bits on "what we learned." It's usually a big hit, and afterwards, many times the client will say something like, "That was great because it reminds people of what we learned!" Even though I was joking about a lot of it, it still drives the points home. People remember funny things past the event, so sum up a serious point with humor and you'll make a more lasting impression.

NOTE

At a show for university food service people who had a session on the cafeteria's new initiative to go "trayless" (as in no trays). "So your schools are going trayless? What are the students going to use as sleds? When I went to Virginia Tech, we used to steal trays to sled down the hill. I miss those days, you know—when my rear end could fit on a tray!"

Humor Sells.

I once heard that the biggest motivators to do anything are fear, pride and material gain, but they forgot humor. Have we learned nothing from the Super Bowl commercials? Humor sells. Period. Those ads cost millions of dollars for a mere minute and the majority of 'em are funny, or trying to be, because advertisers realize that if you're laughing during the game, you might be talking about their products around the water cooler the next day.

Humor Makes You Likeable and Approachable.

I have CEOs come up to me after the show, when I've had their permission to poke fun at them, and say things like, "That was great, because now everyone in my company sees that I can take a joke, and I look more approachable." That's a good thing—unless you don't want anyone in the company to approach you! (Maybe you're the IT person? Kidding!) Even if your humor isn't belly-laugh funny, making a wisecrack or two lets people know that you're one of the "good guys." It disarms you to your staff, clients, patients, coworkers and the rest of the world.

Humor Stops Stress and Relaxes People.

Or so everyone tells me. I still get stressed, but at least I can joke about it. Lots of humorists out there will tell you how humor relieves stress. They're absolutely right. I don't know the exact things it does inside your body, but I do know that when you're laughing, it's hard to feel stressed. And when others are stressed, if you can crack a joke, it'll relax them.

And those of you in those scary "helping" professions like nurses, doctors, dentists, hygienists and the like can really benefit by spicing up your small talk with some funny tales. I still remember the funny poster in my dentist's office as a kid: "You don't have to brush all of your teeth, just the ones you want to keep!"

NOTE

I once was introduced as a speaker who will get you to "de-stress." "Hey, if I don't help you de-stress, then may I suggest a second glass of wine?"

Humor Sets the Tone and Changes the Mood.

As a comedian, I sometimes have to use humor to change the mood in the room so people get in the mood for comedy. At some conventions I'm put at the weirdest places in the program. They think comedy can go *anywhere*. Once a group I was performing for had a really big production of lighting candles for each member who had died. Then they brought me up right after the ceremony! Luckily, it was a group I knew I could joke around with, and there were some candles left over. So I kicked off with, "Hey, we've got some candles left. You know what that means, don't you? Some of you weren't supposed to be here. Did anyone get a weird look at registration?" It got a huge laugh and let the crowd move on. If I had just started right in on my jokes, people may not have been ready or may have thought I was ignoring their reverent ceremony. I don't recommend segueing from death to comedy (and you really need to know the group before you say a line like that), but it can be done.

Even if the topic's not death, I might have to follow a speaker who has killed the atmosphere. On one occasion, I did a show for a real estate company at their awards banquet. That year they had just laid off a bunch of people, and the CEO went up ahead of me, and for *10 minutes* talked about how this year has been tough, and so they were toning down the "glitz and glamour" at this awards banquet. He kept repeating the phrase "toning down the glitz and glamour." And he was right, they had toned it down. At the previous year's banquet, they'd had bands and dancing and decorations and cash machines just shooting 20s into the air. (OK, I'm kidding about the 20s, but you get the picture.) This year they literally had folding chairs and a sandwich buffet. And here's the CEO right before me, pounding home the point. What do you think the mood was as I walked on stage? I had to do something to change it, so I came up with my opening line on the fly: "Wow, Bob said we're toning down the glitz and glamour, and then he introduces me, like I'm the blandest speaker you could find." That got a nice laugh and it gave everyone permission to have some fun and relax and, more importantly, it changed the mood!

Humor Breaks the Ice.

You've got to start your conversation, speech or letter somehow. You might as well tell a joke, make a funny observation or say something other than, "Hi. How are you?" Get people laughing and you'll get 'em engaged right away, so that you at least have a shot at getting them to listen to the rest of your message. My sister Brenda once started a speech in college with, "My dad always told me to start a speech with a joke. Well, I've never listened to his advice before and I'm not going to now." And then she went into her speech. Funny.

Humor Gets You Free Stuff.

Hey, you can scream at the waiter because he overcooked your steak and you'll get a free steak. But if you joke with him, you might get a free steak *and* he won't let his dog lick the steak first! I have never waited tables, but I just know that's what they do! Try joking around when things aren't going your way, and people just may go out of their way to help you.

Humor Gets Your Point Across.

The saying "Many a truth is said in jest" is true. You can say something that's true and make the point with humor and people will get the message. "Hey, Joe, is deodorant out of the budget this month?" OK, maybe that's a little harsh, but we all can use a little humor to get our points across. Humor also helps validate your point of view. One of the cool benefits comics get from telling jokes they've written is that they get validation from and connect with people who see the comic's point of view. It's sort of like the comic saying, "Here's where I'm coming from. Am 1 a nut or does anyone else think this is weird?" When the audience "gets it," you don't feel so isolated in the world. Other people really are thinking like you do.

NOTE

Humor helps you poke tasteful fun at people, places and things: "When you manage people you learn a lot of stuff—like most relatives die on Fridays."

Humor Gets You out of Embarrassing Situations.

Our bodies make noises at inappropriate times, we trip walking on a totally flat surface, and we find out our zipper is down when we get home after two hours of shopping. What do we do about it? We tend to ignore what just happened, the big elephant in the room, when, in fact, people are going to laugh anyway. You might as well say something funny and put yourself and everyone at ease. Maybe people will focus on your joke instead of your social faux pas.

Humor Gets People to Do What You Want Them to Do.

Probably because of all of the above reasons, humor is persuasive. Magicians, hypnotists and others who need to get people on stage do it by joking with audience members. Hey, if they came right out and said, "Who wants to come up here so I can put you in a trance that'll make you walk like a chicken and be a fool?" well, nobody would ever raise their hand.

Why Not Use Humor?

What's the worst thing that could happen if you try to use humor? You never hear people say, "Wow, Bob tried to tell a joke. It was awful. I hate him!" Unless you told a really bad, off-color/inappropriate joke (We'll get to appropriate humor later.) or they paid money in a comedy club to see you telling jokes and, well, you didn't. Then you've got a problem. Otherwise, *most* people will appreciate that you're trying to lighten things up. And even lame humor still has many of the benefits mentioned above. We'll address "bombing" later, but don't let the possibility of having a flat line keep you from spicing up your communications. People are generally grateful for the effort.

Plus, when you're looking to make things fun, it just makes life a little more interesting for you. Whether you're dealing with the public as a customer service rep, trying to sell a product or speaking at a staff meeting, don't you think you would at least be more interesting to yourself if you found ways to be funny?

So that's the short list of why you should inject some hilarity into your communications. There are lots of other reasons, but I'd rather move on to "the how" than spend time with "the why." I hate going to a seminar on how to get rich, and they spend 90 percent of the time telling me why I want to be rich. I already know that. So tell me how! With that said, let the fun(ny) begin!

CHAPTER

GETTING INSIDE THEIR HEADS

Whether the subject is credit cards, insurance or widgets, get into your customers' or your audiences' heads to find the funny fast.

One of the quickest ways to put humor into conversations, speeches and documents is to put yourself in other people's shoes and say or write what they are probably thinking. It'll most likely come out funny. We all have a little sarcastic voice in our heads, don't we? It's not just comedians. When you were disciplined by your parents, you had a comeback for mom or dad, right? You just didn't say it because you wanted to *live*. Well now's the time to use that voice!

Picking the Right Thought for Funny.

One technique I use a lot when writing on the fly at conventions, is looking and listening to the environment and then voicing what the people in the audience are probably thinking. Was there a speaker who made a comment that you can play off of? Did something happen at the convention that everyone is talking about? Is the room cold or hot? Does it have high ceilings or low ceilings, or is it really long? Give some thought to what the people you're in front of are thinking to themselves about the situation.

That's what happened at the "glitz and glamour" incident I mentioned earlier. Right before I went on stage, after the CEO had "warmed up" the crowd by telling them how he was toning down the "glitz and glamour," I ran through a whole list in my head based on what those people were probably thinking because of that opening. Here's what I came up with:

- Wow, he just reminded me of all the people we just laid off.
- Should I be looking for a new job?
- I guess I should be thankful for the measly buffet and soda he's giving us.
- All the speakers (and, in fact, this whole party) are going to be *boring*.

Well, I couldn't use the first line because that sets the tone for un-fun. Let's not bring up again the reasons for the crappy food, cheap decorations and all the layoffs. And I certainly didn't want to remind them that they should probably be looking for new jobs! That was too close to the truth, in my opinion. And making fun of the food probably would not endear me to the CEO. So my fourth alternative—to take what the guy said *literally* and apply it to myself—seemed like a great option! So that's what I did. And also, by making fun of myself, I got the audience on my side quickly. (Making fun of yourself is one of the tips mentioned later.) Now, some speakers might say that you shouldn't suggest to the audience that you might be boring. But I know I'm *not* boring, and you shouldn't be either if you're speaking to a group, which means you *should* be able to have some fun with the audience's expectations of you!

NOTE

Kids say what we're thinking all the time, don't they? They haven't developed filters like adults, so they just blurt out what they, and usually we adults, are thinking, good or bad. I went to a Mexican restaurant with my brother and his family. My 10-year-old nephew, Patrick, ordered the Fiesta Platter, which by the way, was the size of Mexico. It was huge! So the check came, I grabbed it, and my brother tried to grab it, and we're doing that tussle thing over who pays, when Patrick blurts out, "Dad, let her have it. We don't know how much this thing cost!"

Listening to the Sarcastic Voice.

Whatever the communication is, written or oral, if you can get inside people's heads and say what the audience (be it one person or 1,000 people) is sarcastically thinking, then you'll start with a laugh and have their attention. I once followed an awards ceremony in which the employees gave their boss a plaque and listed all the reasons she deserved this award, including that she was the most trustworthy and honest person in the company. What a great opening line for me! "Hey, your employees just admitted that they aren't *that* honest!"

Even if you're not at a convention, you can still pay attention to what the other person's voice is saying. Are you a nurse having to do some embarrassing procedure to a patient? Are you an insurance agent meeting with a new client? Are you a CEO writing a memo about the company's state of the union? Look at it from someone else's point of view, and think about what they're thinking.

If I were networking and heard the CEO talking about no more "glitz and glamour," I'd be looking for signs of glitz and glamour (jewelry, nice shoes, etc.) on everyone I met to give me an ice breaker line such as "Hey, I love your shoes. You're going to get in trouble because they're a little too glitzy and glamorous for us today."

Acknowledging Your Role.

I've already showed you how you can listen to speakers ahead of you and play off of them. But what if *you* are the opening speaker? I recently worked with a CEO who told me he once had to give a speech in front of Bill Gates. So you know the audience is really waiting for Bill Gates. What do you think is in their heads when this CEO walks out to do the "warm up" speech? If I were in that position, I would've acknowledged the fact that everyone is waiting for Gates by saying something like, "I know I'm not Bill Gates (what everyone is thinking). If I were I wouldn't be *here*. I'd be on a beach somewhere drinking a margarita!"

This is a slight modification of what some comedians do when they're opening for a band. The audience doesn't want to hear the comedian. They want Bruce Springsteen or whatever group they spent 180 bucks to see. So sometimes the comic starts off with not so much a joke but more of an acknowledgement of what's to come: "Hey, I was backstage hanging out with Bruce and he's really psyched about coming on stage." That gives the audience the impression that this comic is a buddy of Bruce's, and that Bruce thinks he's cool, so the audience should listen to him.

Often I'm sandwiched on the agenda between some really technical or esoteric talks. This gives me a great line to kick off the show with: "So I took a look at your agenda and thought, Wow, I don't have to be all that funny to be more entertaining than this! If you're having trouble sleeping tonight, may I suggest you read the agenda." Even if the meeting isn't boring, the names of the sessions can sound dull and confusing, and many of the attendees are wondering if I really am going to be funny, so pointing out that I promise to be funnier than their agenda is, well, funny.

Using This Technique if You're Writing a Sales Letter.

What do you think people think when they get yet *another* sales letter? It amazes me how many boring letters credit card companies come up with when they're trying to lure you into using those checks that cost a million dollars in interest. Their letters are all the same! Wouldn't you like one of them to just say what we're thinking? Of course, they're not going to come right out and say, "Hey, these checks are a scam. Use 'em," or "Use these checks and we both make money!" But how about a little humorous honesty? The people who use those checks can't get money and need cash fast. How about, "Let's face it, the car insurance is due and you need the dough. Use these checks so your payment is on time and your credit score is safe for another month." People who don't need the cash aren't going to use the checks anyway, let alone read the letter. And people who need the cash will probably appreciate some humor.

NOTE

When was the last time you read a sales letter that made you laugh?

Using This Technique Talking to People One-on-One.

Put yourself in the other person's shoes during one-on-one chats, and you'll come up with some funny. I was going from Los Angeles up to Santa Barbara with a friend of mine for a day trip. It's a two-hour Amtrak ride, and if you've ever ridden on Amtrak, you know that you get your ticket but you don't get your seat assignment until you're boarding—at least that's the deal with the cheap seats we bought. So when you're boarding, you hand the conductor your ticket and he hands you a seat assignment. Well, the guy in front of us was just dancing around, very hyper, and he kept going on and on, right in the conductor's face, about how he wanted to sit in the club car (you know, where they serve the booze).

He was practically yelling this mantra, "I want to sit in the club car, I want to sit in the club car," and the poor conductor was just flustered. Finally, the conductor finished with him and sent him onto the train. Well I'm behind the guy and I'm thinking, "Man, what's this poor conductor thinking?" I ran through a few ideas of what must be going through his head. So when I got up to the conductor, I blurted out, "Man, you think that guy needs a drink? Forget the club car, I think he needs the Ritalin car! Wouldn't it be funny if the club car was closed?" The conductor started laughing and he gave us great ocean-view seats. That, by the way, is how you get free stuff; ok, special treatment in this case, but you get the picture!

NOTE

Say what the other person is thinking and you'll change the energy from stressful to positive in seconds. When we took my sister to the hospital, we got through the whole situation using humor. In the emergency room we noticed that people who were bleeding got in first. Which led to the observation, "I figured out the system in the emergency room. The person who is bleeding gets to the top of the list. My sister was at the bottom because she wasn't bleeding . . . at first. After five hours of waiting, I said, 'Debbie, I've got to cut you.'"

Even when you're talking one-on-one to someone over the phone, if you can put yourself in their shoes and say what they're thinking, you'll probably get a laugh. I've done a lot of cold calling, and, believe me, when you're the "product," it's hard to sell unless you've got a sense of humor! I think I'd rather sell something I don't have such a high stake in. But I have to make the calls, and because I'm selling the fact that I'm funny, I'd better be able to put my mouth where my, er, ah, mouth is. I don't start off with a joke, but I do try to say what they're thinking when I sense some resistance or, worse, if I mess up my pitch. I have stumbled over words a few times, and I immediately stop and say what the person is thinking. "Hey, a speaker who can't speak!" or, "I can't speak today. Must be because I'm not getting paid."

Saying what the other person is thinking is fun, whether you're trying to get a good seat on Amtrak, or you work with patients in a hospital or even when you're on the front lines of customer service. You can beat an angry customer to the punch when you say what their sarcastic voice is thinking. It'll definitely take the air out of their tires and probably change the mood to something more positive.

Using This Technique for General Written Correspondence.

If you're sending out a memo on the "state of the company," what do you think the recipients are sarcastically thinking when they get it? Instead of opening with "Our company's vision statement, blahhhhhh, snoorrceee . . ." Try kicking it off with something that'll grab 'em, because they're probably thinking:

- I need to grab some caffeine so I can stay awake!
- Perfect timing! I'm out of cat litter liners.
- This is going in the circular file.

So why not jolt them awake with something funny? Make a list of 20 things you know they'd rather do than read this memo or 20 things you know they're going to do with the memo *after* they've read it, or just blurt out some funny, off-the-wall, outrageous advantage they'll get if they read it, like losing weight or curing baldness.

At some of my jobs, I've used humor in correspondence to get people to act on something I wanted them to do. I was in charge of membership for an association in which about 300 members were actually paying the much cheaper student member dues rate instead of the regular member dues rate—and they'd been members for, oh, 20 years or more. I wanted these people to come clean, so I drafted a tongue-in-cheek letter that began, "While we here at X association do believe in lifelong learning, you have taken it just a little too far . . ." OK, my boss wouldn't let me send out that one, but I was successful with yet another tactic, "Dear Student Member, we are profiling all of our student members in the next few issues of the magazine, and we've chosen *you*. I'll be calling in the next few days to go over the details so you can be featured prominently in our student section. . . ." I got a 100 percent conversion rate! And while neither letter kicked off with an outright joke, there was humor in them, and it certainly beat the heck out of just telling these people that we think they're cheating the system and they need to 'fess up. I got inside their heads and thought, what do these people think when they pay their membership dues every year? Probably something like, "Yeah, I'm still passing myself off as a student and nobody knows about it!" Bingo! I had a great opening line.. What if everybody learns about it in the magazine?

The members who got the letter probably appreciated the humor—and the fact that we didn't charge them for their years of deception!

Practice Thinking Like Your Audience.

Luckily, because of bad customer service and lack of patience on the part of most of the population, you can practice saying what the other person is thinking all the time during everyday tasks. That way when it comes to a speech, or when you're trying to come up with a line for a letter or you're struggling for something to say at the cocktail party, it'll be old hat. There are opportunities all around you to practice saying what the other person is thinking.

For example:

When you're standing in line at the bank and the bank teller is dealing with a difficult customer, what do you think the bank teller is thinking? *Say it!* You'll probably get a laugh and they won't mess up your deposit.

Or how about practicing in elevators? This is especially fun to do in casino elevators. When I see people with big empty coin buckets heading up to their rooms, I quip, *"I guess it's time to go up and watch the free TV."*

Or, how about when you call a customer service computer hotline? The poor guy's been there all day answering 90 percent of the same ridiculous questions from people about their computers. *"How do I turn it on?"* *"What's a browser?"* You know, stuff like that. Start the conversation off with what he's probably thinking and you'll get your discussion off on a positive note. Maybe he'll even skip the part about rebooting your computer, like you hadn't tried that one already!

Remember, It's Their Sarcastic Voice, Not Yours!

It's important to say what you think *the other person* is thinking, not what *your* little sarcastic voice is saying. *That* will not get you free stuff! In fact that won't even come off as funny, but rather you might just infuriate whomever you're dealing with. I had a problem with the post office once when they were messing up one of my mailings. Now, if you work for the P.O., don't get all defensive on me. I absolutely love our mail service, and I *usually* have no problems with the post office—except for this one time. The 250 pieces I had mailed were coming back to me, and the postal clerk and I were trying to figure it out. It was getting very frustrating, when finally she just slammed down the mail and blurted out, "This is not my fault!" Well, *my* sarcastic voice wanted to blurt out, *"What's that? The motto of the post office?"* Not a good choice of words. That would not make her my friend and I probably could expect more mail coming back to me. The whole point is to put yourself in *someone else's* shoes. In this case, I was too angry to be funny, so I kept my mouth shut.

CHAPTER

ANALOGIES, STEREOTYPES AND COMMON ASSUMPTIONS, OH MY!

Use common knowledge, even if it's inaccurate
(example: Women are bad drivers.), to get to the funny fast.

Another way I write humor fast is by making connections between elements in the environment and stereotypes, common assumptions and analogies we have about those elements. The only time you're allowed to use stereotypes and common assumptions is when writing and speaking comedy—and then, only as long as you're *nice*.

When I walk into a room where I'm speaking, I make a list, either on paper or in my head, of all the things in the environment. Who's in the room? Is it cold? Is it hot? Are there decorations? What's the seating like? And then I take one of those elements and list common assumptions, stereotypes and analogies about it.

NOTE

Have some fun with common stereotypes we have about people. For example, the rich: "Bill Gates threw a top-secret party on an Alaskan cruise ship for 500 of the world's most famous people, including many top models. For the first time, there was more saline on a ship than in the water."

For example, if I see 700 women in the room, which is one of the elements in the environment, I then list all of the analogies, stereotypes and common assumptions (even if they aren't exactly accurate) that people have about women. Women talk a lot, carry big purses, take a long time in the bathroom, have PMS, bash men, wear a lot of makeup and are not good drivers.

Then I make a connection between the element in the environment (women) and the common assumption, analogy or stereotype (long time in the bathroom) we have about that element to come up with a joke such as, "It's nice to be here with 700 women, but I've been trying to get into the bathroom since 6:30 this morning." Or, "I knew there were a lot of women at this event. All the cars in the parking lot have dents." All right that one's easier to get away with *if* you're a woman. (We'll get into some of the rules for using humor later.) And again, the stereotype may not be correct. (I think women are actually *better* drivers than men.) It just has to be the collective viewpoint.

Another example: Suppose you walk in and it's really *freezing*. I mean so cold that everyone feels it, so you've got to say something. Come up with things that everyone associates with cold. You can start with the obvious stuff, which is usually not that funny, but it'll get you warmed up, so to speak. Things we associate with cold include the sniffles, Mt. Everest, snow, refrigerators, Eskimos, ice cream, ice cubes.

Then ramp it up a bit. Take the opposite of things we associate with cold—things we associate with hot. Anything funny? The devil, hot flashes/menopause, sweating. Get outrageous. Ask what's cold? Where is it cold? Who is cold? Step over the line if you have to; you can always come back. Who is cold? Naked people, people who live in Iceland, my ex-husband/wife, the Clintons' bedroom. (Not being political, just trying to be funny—and political figures are fair game!)

Ahhhh, now we're getting somewhere. "Boy it's freezing in here! Who's in the audience? My ex-wife?" Or, "Hey, this place is colder than the Clinton bedroom."

Now try it again with another element of the environment. Maybe the ceilings are high. What does everyone associate with high? When do we associate with high? Who do we associate with high? Where do we associate with high? Again, get outrageous and you can come up with things, like, the sky, birds, Ozzy Osbourne. This might lead you to, "Hey, the ceilings in here are almost as high as Ozzy Osbourne."

The cool thing about referencing the environment when talking with someone or in giving a speech is that you don't need to use a lot of words to do it. You don't have to say, "It's freezing," because people in that environment know it's freezing. Start out looking at the stuff closest and easiest, like the room set up if you're physically present. And then move out from there to the entire hotel, the city, the state.

Using the Environment When You're Not Present.

But what about if you're writing a sales letter and you're not physically in the environment? You can still figure out what's in your audience's environment by pulling together what you know about them, and then connecting it with analogies, stereotypes and common assumptions. And, depending on how much time you want to spend, you can do as little or as much research as you want.

I write a lot of material for conventions in advance, when I'm not in the environment yet, or for TV/radio or some other media in which I'll never be in the environment. Since I'm not physically anywhere but in my office, I have to gather a little bit of information or do a little more pondering to figure out the common things that people can relate to. Comedy is all about having a common experience. People are funny at the water cooler because the people at the water cooler have common experiences. If your group isn't physically at the water cooler, then you have to find out what links them and pull the humor from that.

Obviously, you can't make a crack about high ceilings because not everybody reading your letter shares that. But maybe you're selling life insurance to new parents. Ask yourself what are our stereotypes about insurance? It's necessary. It's scary. People buy it out of fear. It's boring.

Now what are some of the common things (environmental elements) that new parents share? Screaming infants, wet diapers, late nights, babies who keep us awake at night. Eureka! Babies are awake and insurance is perceived as boring!

Do you see a connection? Maybe something like, "Buy our insurance and give this letter to your baby. Then you'll both sleep at night." OK, corny, but you get the picture.

Start by making your lists:

- What do you know about the people you're writing for or speaking to—age, sex, other characteristics?
- What are stereotypes, common assumptions or analogies associated with their age, gender, profession?
- What are the stereotypes, common assumptions and analogies associated with your product?

Here's a quick list of things you might want to know about your audience/readers in order to come up with some common environmental elements:

Age.

Are the people you're writing for and/or speaking to young, old or in the middle? Can you have some fun with the common assumptions we have about people in that age group? What do they remember, and what stereotypes do we have about that age group? For example, if they're in their 60s, what are some things they're dealing with, and what are some of the things we associate with people in their 60s? What are the stereotypes we have about people in their 60s?

- grown kids
- grandkids
- retirement/leaving their jobs
- traveling
- spending their kids' inheritance
- crabbiness—Get off my grass!
- hippies

You might come up with a health insurance sales letter to the effect of: "Our prescription plan is so good, you'll spend less money on drugs now than you did in the 60s."

Ok, don't get yourself fired with drug references, but give some thought to what you can have fun with instead of taking the usual, boring route.

Gender.

If you're writing a sales letter or a memo to a group that's all one gender, the same things apply as if you were physically in front of them. You can have some fun with stereotypes and common assumptions about men or women. I once wrote a joke for radio based on a story in *Redbook* magazine that said men enjoy fixing stuff around the house. I keyed in on "men fixing stuff" and then listed things that could be fixed and things that men (stereotypically) like and don't like to fix. I came up with: "According to *Redbook* magazine, men really enjoy fixing stuff around the house . . . as long as it doesn't involve the word *relationship*."

Geography.

Is your audience in the same region? What common assumptions do we have about certain areas of the country? If your clients are in Minnesota and you're sending out a sales letter in January, then you can have some fun with the cold. What are things we associate with cold and what are stereotypes about your product?

Headaches or Challenges They Face.

Make a list of the challenges that people in your audience face. Then ask if there are some analogies you can make between these challenges and your product or whatever you're writing or speaking about. Or maybe there are stereotypes we have about these challenges that you can have some fun with. Try to think of unique challenges and headaches, not just things like "budget problems," because everyone has those. Be as specific as you can.

I wrote jokes for a group of salespeople who deal with schools, and I found out that one of their biggest headaches was PTA moms. But not that the moms could be a pain in the butt, which was what I first thought I would make jokes about. Rather than their personalities, the bigger challenge was that the PTA mom leaders changed every year. So every year, the salespeople had to start all over schmoozing different contacts. So I made my list of groups that change and groups that don't change every year to see if I could come up with an analogy. That gave me a joke along the lines of, "I've done shows in prisons, but you guys have it tougher because you have to deal with PTA moms. At least the next year, the same prisoners are still there." And even though it may not sound that funny to you, it got a great laugh with them because everyone could connect with it. And making a connection between prisoners and PTA moms is funny!

Knowing headaches and challenges for the group has been a real lifesaver when I've had to come up with comedy on the fly during my program. Once I had to stop a show in front of 2,000 nurses to get a woman to stop videotaping me. Of course, when I stopped and asked her to turn off the camera, there was dead silence. Luckily, I'd done my homework and knew that one of the biggest challenges that nurses have is working around doctors. Most doctors are great, but I was told that there was a bit of tension between nurses and doctors. So I looked at the crowd and came back with, "I don't know how you discipline a nurse. Call her bad names like 'doctor'?" It got a huge laugh and the audience moved on. Had I lost my temper or just tried to go right back into my material without making a connection, it would've been a long 60 minutes.

> ## NOTE
>
> Understanding jobs and the activities people engage in on the job can lead to some fast funny: "So you all work for a meat-packing plant and they make you take sexual harassment training? Just how pretty are these cows?"

Types of Jobs They Do.

Ask yourself, "What are some of the daily activities of the people I'm speaking AND writing for?" Find out what they are dealing with. When I did a show for printers, I found out that one of the most popular (and most expensive) pieces of equipment they use is the Heidelberg press. Humm, that's German. What else do I know that's German or that Heidelberg reminds me of? The Hindenburg! What if I had a Hindenburg press? What would it do? Which led me to the joke: "I know a lot of you guys own the Heidelberg press. My uncle Eddy is a printer, but he's kinda cheap. He bought the Hindenburg press. The first week he had it, it burst into flames."

If it's one particular group, say lawyers, then step through their daily routines to make connections between their activities and stereotypes of lawyers, such as they bill in 12-minute increments; they sue; they spend time in court; they chase ambulances.

Job Titles.

Are you writing for or speaking to a group of people who all have the same job title? If so, can you have some fun with a play on their title or stereotypes we associate with that title, especially if the title is peculiar? And trust me, there are some odd titles out there. I once wrote a joke for a hospital after

I found out that an employee had the title of "sterilization technician." What do we associate with sterilization? What are some of our common assumptions?

- No kids
- Lots of kids
- Ouch

- Quick procedure
- A procedure we do to animals
- Scary

"Hey, she's a Sterilization Technician. Wouldn't it be funny if she had 10 kids?" or, "She's a Sterilization Technician. How does she get a date with that title?" Ask questions and use common assumptions about sterilization and you'll find tons of funny.

I once followed a speaker from the department of health. OK, what do we think of when we hear "department of health"? Diseases, closing down restaurants, washing hands. This led me to: "Hey, no offense everyone, but she's the only person I feel really comfortable shaking hands with." And, "Of course, we didn't know she was here. The manager refused to put up a sign announcing that a woman from the Department of Health was in the hotel!"

Just remember, whether you're in the room physically or you're writing to a group, the environment is everything: the temperature of the room; the way the place is set; where the room is physically located; the agenda; the food; the lighting; the people's age, gender, job titles; the activities they are involved in; their challenges; the other speakers. *Everything* you can think of is fair game.

When you've figured out what you want to focus on in the environment, ask questions and you'll get great answers.

A Thing About Questions.

In writing comedy, and especially in writing *fast* comedy, questions are a huge key. Ask yourself the who, what, when, where, and why of something and you'll come up with many

> ## NOTE
>
> Remember, a lot of what you're trying to do with comedy is to say something without saying it. If you want to say someone is old, then list things commonly associated with old—John McCain, the Magna Carta, Rome.
>
> And then make your connection in the form of an analogy: "I won't say he's old, but he babysat John McCain."

jokes. We started off with one big question: What is the other person thinking? And we kept going with other questions to pull out the funny. Questions make you think differently, so run all the environmental elements (age, gender, temperature,) through the "who, what, when, where, why and how" to get creative. When talking about cold, if you just ask, "What's cold?" you'll get things that aren't so funny. When you ask, "Who's cold?" you'll tap into funny. Or why is it cold? Hummm. . . Why would it be cold in the room? What reasons would the company have for keeping the conference room cold? Ask yourself, "Who benefits from the cold?" And keep looking at your lists to make connections such as:

- The company has added a new frostbite plan to the health insurance and they want to try it out.
- The boss is an Eskimo and he's homesick.
- The fridge broke and we don't want our lunches to spoil.
- The company retreat is on Mt. Everest, so we're getting everyone acclimated.

During the Q&A in my *Finding the Funny in Communications* program, a woman said she worked in customer service for a newspaper and she had to answer calls from people whose newspapers were late or missing. She said she wanted to develop some humor to diffuse the situation. OK, ask yourself the main question, "What could have happened to the paper?" Then answer the question with outrageous answers. Think wacky.

- Your dog ate it. (Funny, but typical. You get to this answer by asking, "What's a standard answer for losing something?")

- *My* dog ate it. (Funnier. You get to this by asking, "What's a twist on the standard answer for losing something?")

- We've been watching your house and we think your neighbor took it. (A little funnier. You get this by asking, "Who else would want the paper?")

- I took it. Sorry. (You get this by asking, "Who else would want the paper?")

Another question: What can you do now that they don't have a paper? Think sarcastic. How else could they get the news?

- We have a new program where I will read you the entire paper. (You get this by asking, "What can I personally do to help her?")

- I can give you the highlights: Britney Spears got drunk. The ladies on *The View* had an argument, etc. Come up with stuff that we *always* read about. (You get this by asking, "What news is she really missing out on?")

Keep going with questions: Why did she not get a paper? Think off the wall.

- There wasn't any news today. (You get this by asking, "Why would there not be a paper?")

- We just wanted to hear from you and this was the only way we could get you to call us. (You get this by asking, "What's good about not getting a paper?")

- There is no more ink in the world. (You get this by asking, "Why would there not be a paper?")

If you have a job where you keep getting repetitive questions, and you want to be funny (*not* a smart alec, just having fun), then prepare ahead of time by writing down some of the common questions people ask, then ask yourself some questions about those questions, and you'll come up with some great lines. Once you have some fun lines, you can use them over and over again, just like comics who write an act and stick with it for a lifetime!

And when you have lots of questions, you'll come up with lots of lists!

A Word About Lists.

Aside from questions, lists are the other key to fast comedy success. When you make lists about things in the environment and their stereotypes, common assumptions, and analogies, it's almost like connecting the lines in those newspaper games where you have two columns and you draw lines between the things that match in the columns. Combining questions and lists forces you to dig deep, be imaginative and really think from different angles, which gives you ammunition for finding the funny *fast*. I've been writing for more than 16 years, so making connections is automatic for me. When I walk into a room or sit down to write for a client, I'm always making a list of things and their related analogies, stereotypes and common assumptions. If you get into this habit, too, you'll write faster and faster.

Go With Your First Impressions.

I think first impressions are huge when writing comedy. If you think too much about it, you'll write a joke that people have to, well, think too much about to get. But if you go with what socks you in the face first, then you can (usually) be assured that others will pick up on it quickly as well. So with your lists, try to go with first impressions and quick word associations. I used to play a game as a kid where someone would shout a word and we'd say the first thing that comes to mind. It wasn't of much use as a kid, but popping off with the first thing that comes to mind is useful when writing comedy.

I do this when I'm not in the actual environment as well. When I sit down to write, I make sure I have all of my notes

NOTE

If you're walking into a room, what is your first impression? This is taking the environment a little further by getting a feel for the room itself. Is the feel of the room creepy? Is the room cluttered with junk? What is the atmosphere? I once did a show where there were all these "antiques" lying around, so I wrote down my list of what I felt while standing in the room. Things that came to mind included grandma's house, the Goodwill store, and a yard sale. And I went with, "Hey, this is the first time I've ever performed at a yard sale."

together *first*. Then I look them over once and take a quick first impression of things that pop out at me. I know it's in my gut reaction and first impression where I'll find the funny. For this reason, if I'm interviewing a client about their group, I never go to their website beforehand and learn all I can about them. I want to go into the conversation somewhat naïve so that I can really listen to what they say and make inexperienced connections. If I do educate myself about the client's business before talking with them, then I tend not to ask the right questions. My brain fills in the blanks with, "Oh, I know that and that and that," and so I'll miss out on some funny material. In the case of the fundraising executives and the PTA moms, if I had stopped the conversation because I thought PTA moms themselves were a pain, then I never would have found out that it's not their personalities but the fact that they change leadership positions every year that poses the problem.

CHAPTER

PULL OUT THE IRONY.

For a credit union show: "I understand your credit union just bought up a whole bunch of those quick, advance loan places that charge 50 percent interest. Your president said it would increase your potentiul membership base by 1 million people . . . who have 30 bucks between 'em."

OK, so you've got your list of the elements in the environment and you also know a bit about the age, sex, and job titles of your audience members. The next way to get to the humor quickly is to look at your environment list and pull out the ironies between two things in the environment or the contradictions and inconsistencies among several things on your lists.

For example, I do a lot of shows for medical groups, and one thing I almost always see at medical conventions when I walk up to the convention center or hotel is smokers out front. That's a big inconsistency—smokers/medical. So I've got my perfect opening line: "Hey, I walked up to the building and I saw all these smokers out front. I thought, 'Yep, I'm at the right place, *these* are the medical people!'" It gets a huge laugh and it's a great way to start off the program. In fact, now I don't even look for smokers at a medical conference because I *know* they're out there. I just say the line and it hits.

If you're not physically in the room, ask yourself what you know about the group and their environment. Who's in the group? What are their job titles? What are their challenges? I wrote a joke for financial planners when I was told that their oldest member who was still working was 86 years old. The irony just jumps out at you! An 86-year-old financial planner? That's not what you want to see in your financial planner. What does that say to the guy's clients? "Hey, he took his own advice. He can't retire!"

Some of the quick things I look at for ironies (these are especially helpful and fast when I'm physically present at an event) are . . .

The Agenda.

The agenda always has great stuff on it that you can have fun with. At one conference where I spoke, the agenda had the following programs:

- Tips for Being Frugal
- Do-It-Yourself Projects
- How to Stay Safe from Identity Theft
- Help Isn't a Four-Letter Word

Now what are the ironies or inconsistencies between any two sessions? This might lead you to humor such as:

- Does anyone see a big irony between tips on being frugal and identity theft? Hey, I think now I know how to be frugal—or at least how not use my own money!

- How much did you guys have to pay for that session on being frugal?

- Go ahead and do it yourself. If that doesn't work out, then remember help is not a four-letter word!

And, the agenda may not stop with you, so comment if you're holding the audience up from something, such as, "I'm the only thing standing between you and happy hour," or "you and rush hour traffic" or "you and the buffet lunch."

The agenda is usually full of ironies. And don't tell me that the sample agenda above happens to be a special circumstance. I guarantee 95 percent of the agendas I've seen have some fun, ironic stuff on them, because the person putting the agenda together is too close to the subject to step back and see the funny. I did a show once where a speaker was talking about his book, *Never Eat Lunch Alone,* and right after his talk—I mean, immediately after it—the agenda said, "Lunch, on your own." The fast funny is on the agenda, trust me.

The Food.

Now you don't want to go making too much fun of the food, but you can goof around a little with it; everything from the look of the food, to the amount of food to when it's served can contribute to some laughs.

Ask yourself questions like, "Why is this food at this conference?" and you'll get some funny answers.

Is every booth giving out candy—at a dental convention?

One time during the luncheon, we had a fashion show. Who sees the irony in that? Let's see, a fashion show involves clothes, makeup and skinny models. That's nice. Models who haven't had a meal since last Tuesday are staggering around while we stuff ourselves.

And many times it's the names of the foods that are funny. I did a show for food service people at universities in which I was reminded of my days at Virginia Tech where we were served "Beef Butterfly." Yes, they paired a meat with an insect and fed it to us!

Also, the types and amount of food served can be ironic. Are there cheese cubes or cookies at every break? "Hey, they feed you all day here. It's the same thing they do to people in prison—fatten you up so you don't try to escape."

And of course the type of food is funny. I've done tons of shows for women's groups and they almost always have sessions on being healthy. And then what do they serve you for lunch? Usually some dessert that's about a million calories!

The look of the food is important, too. Chefs get carried away sometimes and make dishes that none of us has ever seen before! Hey, if you don't know what the heck the meat was, chances are, most of the attendees don't either. You can also always make up funny names based on what it looks like, such as "the-cook-is-new special," "the end-of-the-week medley" or "this-has-to-go-now pudding."

As long as you're being (somewhat) nice about it, the food is one common experience that everyone has that will get you to the ironic funny fast.

Events.

Consider events on the agenda that aren't just someone speaking. Maybe there's some teambuilding stuff you can have fun with or some special entertainment. I did a show in Las Vegas and they kicked off the convention by having some seventh graders sing. The woman speaking ahead of me raved about the kids and how wholesome it was to have them sing at the convention. So I had my mental list of the environment, including "kids" and "Vegas," which gave me a great ironic opening line: *"Wholesome? Seventh graders singing in a casino?* Apparently you guys have a different definition of wholesome!"

I've also had some fun with teambuilding exercises and their placement on the agenda. During one meeting, the attendees beat drums and shook rattles as a form of—well, I don't know what they were shooting for—teambuilding, I guess. But it was followed by a talk on professionalism. "Hey, I think we should've had the professionalism talk *before* everyone got hold of those rattles!"

Giveaways.

Look at the giveaways they have for attendees either in the exhibit hall or at registration, and find inconsistencies and ironies with those. I spoke at a women's convention once where they gave everyone a grooming kit. We're at a convention. We *think* we're groomed, don't we? And then they hand you that?

So I opened with, "Hey, I'm feeling kinda bad here. Am I the only one who arrived at registration and was immediately given a grooming kit?" Or at one convention, they were trying to be all "green" and environmentally friendly, which seems to be the rage these days, and they gave away solar-powered flashlights. Does anybody see the irony in that? Sometimes this stuff writes itself and you just have to bring it up. "Man, this will work really *great* in the sun! And when the lights go out at night, you'll feel safe reaching for your *solar-powered flashlight!*" I predict this "going green" stuff will provide the next big wave of new material.

NOTE

Kids pull out the irony and inconsistencies all the time, don't they? Because they don't understand things, they ask what sound like uninformed questions and then put two and two together in their heads based on their misunderstanding. My sister Brenda got a speeding ticket with her 5-year-old in the car. After the cop left, her daughter asked, "Mom, how do you know how fast to go?" and my sister said, "Well, there are signs." Her daughter thought for a minute and then said, "Well, can't you read?"

5

CHAPTER

SELF-DEPRECATING HUMOR ROCKS.

I like being single. I've just realized some stuff about single people. We don't update our photographs. My parents have a den full of pictures of my brother and sisters' engagements, weddings, families and kids. I'm still there in my cap and gown. Apparently I peaked at graduation!

Self-deprecating humor is probably the best and safest thing to start out with—and the quickest way to get to a joke and connect with your audience. Much of comedy is about letting the audience feel superior. Starting out with a barb on yourself (true for writing or speaking), puts everyone at ease and lets them feel like you're one of them because you're not perfect either. Here are some quick ways to do self-deprecating humor:

Bring up Something Weird About Yourself that People Don't Know.

I've got a 12-AAA shoe size. You wouldn't know that just by looking at me (thank goodness), so I bring it up. I can make fun of big feet, and I do. People with big feet enjoy it because it's someone else in their boat, and people with smaller feet enjoy it because—Whew!—it's not them! So come up with an interesting fact about yourself, or make one up if you have to. It'll break the ice.

Address What People See First.

If you're really tall or have a really funky hairdo or a big knot on your head, then, for crying out loud, bring it up. If you don't mention it, people will spend the first few minutes thinking, "Does she know she has a big knot on her head?" Comics are always joking about the bad haircut they just got. It's an easy way to connect fast. You don't have to do a bunch of jokes, just one quip to get things rolling.

I have comic friends who have a variety of disabilities from muscular dystrophy to cerebral palsy. They all make at least one joke about it. Some of them spend more time on it and some of them do the joke and move on.

Point Out Who You Remind People Of.

If you look like someone famous or notorious point it out! I happen to look like the actress Meredith Baxter Burney, which gives me a great, self-deprecating opening line for the late-night young comedy club groups. "I know you heard there was a woman comic coming up and now you're disappointed. You were hoping for a hot, sexy, 21-year-old. Instead you get me—the mom from that show *Family Ties*. A lot of comics kick off with a statement that they look like the child of two famous people. It may not be something you would notice right away, but once they say that, you think, "Oh, yeah, she's right. She does look like the child of Mick Jagger and Laura Bush."

NOTE

Make fun of yourself and people will like you! I once performed at a posh resort right after a Tina Turner impersonator. I walked out and said, "Tina was great. I'm going to drag her to the spa tomorrow and scream make me look like that!"

Use an Embarrassing Story.

OK, you don't want to look foolish to people or sound foolish in a letter, but ask yourself if there's something that you have done that didn't turn out so well. Can you connect it to what you're writing or speaking about? If I'm doing a show for financial people, I can have some fun with my inability to balance my checkbook. Or if it's a ritzy hotel for example, I can bring up something funny I did there. "I tried to save money by using those free sample bottles of shampoo in the bathroom. My hair now has that silky feel to it . . . because I've been shampooing with hand lotion."

CHAPTER

JOKE FORMULAS

People recognize joke formulas, so your audience is keyed in to laugh at the right time--if it's funny.

Joke formulas are fast because you can just plug your lists into the formula and, poof! You've got a joke. I've used a lot of joke formulas. Some of my favorites include:

Quick Surveys.

This is a great way to get people engaged *instantly*, and it can also break the ice at an event or staff meeting. Start with a quick, funny survey by asking a rhetorical question. For example, if it's really hot in the room, start with, "Hey, how many people here now know what it's like to work on the sun?" You've made your list of hot stuff and the sun was in there, so just plug it into the formula.

And the cool thing with surveys about the environment is you don't have to use a lot of words. You don't have to say, "It's so hot in here," because people will get it when you reference the sun. I once polled the audience after the CEO spent 40 minutes making a very long-winded analogy between life and the Super Bowl. He apparently spent the entire game (which had just played that week) coming up with these bits of wisdom! After he finished, the audience was a little bleary-eyed, so I kicked off with a quick survey: "Hey, how many people here hope that next year during the Super Bowl, Bob does what the *rest* of us do and just drinks a beer?" Of course, I had his permission to be funny. Don't get yourself in trouble!

Good News/Bad News.

The good news is this is an easy formula. The bad news is people see the joke coming! I've used this in examples earlier, but just to reiterate, it's very easy to take elements and make lists of good and bad things—the more outrageous the better—and put them in this format, and poof! You've got a quick joke. "The bad news is it's freezing in here. The good news is those of you going through menopause won't have to change your shirt three times."

It's More ____ Than ____

Earlier I mentioned that one of the stereotypes about women is that they use a lot of makeup, so you could plug in that stereotype of makeup into this formula to come up with, "There's more makeup in here than . . . than what? What else do people associate with lots of makeup? A Mary Kay factory, Tammy Faye Bakker (RIP), a French hooker (watch yourself!), Bozo the Clown.

He's So . . . Old, Cheap, Fat, Dumb, Crazy . . .

This formula never gets old. Again, just plug in the analogy, and say it without saying it. Take your list of what's crazy, who's crazy, etc, and compare it to the person you're calling crazy. "He's so crazy even bin Laden keeps his distance."

Top Lists.

These became popular with David Letterman, and they still work. We did a ton of them for radio. We called 'em "top" lists, not "top 10" lists because you don't always have 10 items. Maybe you'll come up with a Top Five or Top 20. Many of them kick off with things like:

- Top Reasons . . .
- Top Ways . . .
- Top Signs . . .
- Top Excuses . . .
- Top Things That are Better . . .
- Top Things That are Worse . . .
- Top Things You Don't Want to See . . .

Look at your lists of stereotypes and common assumptions and just plug in the lines. The top three signs I knew there were lots of women here:

1. Long lines in the bathroom
2. Dented cars in the parking lot
3. It smells like a perfume factory.

Or create your list by developing worst case scenarios. For example, when writing "Things You Don't Want to Hear from Your Surgeon," think about everything it takes to be a surgeon—years of school, steady hands, lots of money and all the things he or she does in a day— cuts people open, scrubs hands, writes prescriptions. Based on this, what would be scary? A surgeon with no education or one who has lots of germs. This might lead you to lines such as: "I'll be right with you as soon as I finish framing my GED certificate." Or, "I almost stayed home today, but I thought, 'I'm a professional. One little open sore on my hand is not going to keep me from operating.'"

People are used to seeing these top lists, and they're almost always funny, so if you use one in a sales letter, for example, there's probably a good chance people will read it—and then continue reading the letter.

NOTE

There are other joke formulas out there, but I think these are the quickest to work with. Keep a running list whenever you hear a joke formula you like. Then, once you've got your lists, you can plug in the elements and you're off to the races in minutes.

Rap Songs and Poems.

I've written rap songs and poems on the fly to spice up the usual comedy show. Take a couple of key words from the event or about the group and see what they rhyme with. You can even use the standard "roses are red, violets are blue" poem to spark an idea, or change it to "roses are red, violets are green" if a key word rhymes with green.

7

CALLBACKS ARE COOL.
TAGS ARE TREMENDOUS.

*Making lists will give you several
great punch lines. Use them all!*

Want to do some humor *fast, fast, fast?* Use callbacks and tags. Besides being fast, they are really fun, and they allow you to tie together your speech or letter with a running theme throughout. Callbacks are when you refer back to a previous joke or incident or you reference something that's already been mentioned. Tags are when you go an extra step and find a second punch line.

Making a Connection with Callbacks.

Callbacks are cool because you don't need that many words. You can call back to another speaker's speech, something that happened at the convention, or something that's happening in the industry. Everyone gets it pretty quick. For example, if a speaker before you was talking about how to make cold calls and they harped and harped on *not* calling on Monday, you could start off with a callback such as, "So I was cold calling last Monday . . . " You don't need to say much to get a response because people will get it instantly. If you're going to do that though, *make sure that it's something people will remember* from the previous speaker and/or the speech was right before yours and it's a major point.

I was emceeing a convention once in South Dakota, and the first day I pronounced the state capitol Pierre like the French name. But let me tell you, they pronounce it *Pier*, like what you hook a boat up to, and they let me know it! So I had fun with that the whole week by calling back to it. And even during my comedy show at the end of the convention, when I was talking about my sister's kids, I said my nephew's name was Pier, but he pronounces it Pierre. You get lots of bang for your joke dollar when you can keep the joke running with callbacks.

Extending the Laugh with Tags.

The tag is also a way to get good bang for your joke buck. It can be either a callback that you do right after the joke or a second punch line that is at least as funny as, if not funnier than, the original punch line. My oldest joke, my makeup joke, just keeps going with tags and callbacks:

"I went shopping. I walked into the store and was attacked by the makeup lady. She asked what kind of makeup remover I used. I said, "The pillow." CALLBACK/TAG: "They just scatter when you say stuff like that." TAG/SECOND PUNCHLINE: "Of course, they'll give you a free makeover. They can't do product testing on animals anymore." The first tag is more of a callback to squeeze more laughs out of the original punch line, and the second tag is funny in and of itself and it could probably stand on its own without the first punch line.

I was performing at a probation officers' conference where we watched a movie that had the line, "You'll take this to your fricking grave." We used that line throughout the conference, including at the end, when the client got up after me and said, "I hope you've enjoyed the conference, and that you'll take all the information you learned here *to your fricking grave!*" Hilarious!

So don't get lazy. Once you've got your list of things you associate with something and you find a punch line you like, then keep looking for an even better punch line. You'll surprise yourself. And once you've got your whole speech or document written, look at ways to call back to parts of it. Do a quick search and see if a particular word comes up over and over. If so, then see if you can tie in some quick lines to make the callback.

NOTE

To find callbacks and tags when you're speaking, you must be totally present **mentally**, even if you've said your speech a million times. During my comedy routine, I'm also thinking about the group I'm in front of and what's been happening at the event so I can make some quick connections to my jokes. If you're looking to add a callback or tag when you're writing, when you finish, check the beginning to see if there's some way to wrap it all up by closing with what you opened with.

CHAPTER

FINDING QUICK HUMOR IN OTHER PLACES

Humor is where you find it. Look everywhere.

There's no end to what you can use to get a quick laugh. You need to be open to finding the funny anywhere. Here are a few things you can do to create jokes. I've used all of these successfully.

Twist Adages.

There are tons of familiar sayings—adages, if you will—that you can rearrange to add quick humor. Get yourself a book of them and have some fun by twisting them. Most jokes include a setup with something real and then a twist. If you make a fun twist on a standard adage, you'll suck people into the joke because their brains will be waiting for the standard answer. For example, "It's always darkest before . . . the crap hits the fan," and, "There's always a light at the end of the . . . electric chair."

Play with Terms and Acronyms.

I have yet to run across a group that doesn't use way too many terms and acronyms specific to their organization or industry. It's not just for the government anymore! But that's a good thing, because these terms and acronyms lend themselves perfectly to writing humor fast. Make up a new definition for the term, such as: We're having another reorg, and we all know "reorg" is a Latin term for "musical chairs." Or, make up some definitions of acronyms. What else could the letters spell? I did a program for Air Force personnel in which an acronym IAT (installation acquisition transfer) meant basically a reorg where people would be moved around the country. I redefined IAT as "I Am Traveling" and got a huge laugh.

But how do you come up with funny definitions? Take the acronym and list out what it *represents*. For example in the medical community the acronym CMS—Center for Medicare and Medicaid Services—is the name of the government entity that governs reimbursement for Medicare and Medicaid. For healthcare people it *represents* hours and hours of paperwork, rules and regulations, headaches, a big mess dealing with requirements of the laws. Then think of other words that start with a C, an M and an S that *represent* those ideas. Do this quickly by using your computer's thesaurus. If you put in "mess," for example, the word "confusion" comes up . . . and it starts with a C! Yeah! And you're dealing with medical people—M. And what is all of this? It's stuff—an S! CMS = Confusing Medical Stuff. It sounds like a long process, but it's actually pretty quick if you concentrate for a minute or two on what the term represents and use your thesaurus.

NOTE

You can also string together acronyms in a sentence. I did this for an employment benefits group. Everyone could follow me and they got a kick out of seeing what they must look like to outsiders. "I like listening to you all talk because you have your own special language: We've got a TA on that Zipper clause written by the PERB. I hear it's gonna be tough because they all want a COLA. According to the MMBA if that labor agreement expires, then IOU an MOU and we're gonna have to call in an ALJ to deal with all this BS—that's Bargaining Stuff. And we need to do this ASAP or we're gonna be SOL—that's Sortta Outta Luck!"

Use Facts and Figures.

Facts and figures are easy to use in a joke. If you find out 60 percent of people do one thing, for example, then turn it around and ask yourself, what do the other 40 percent do? Or why is it *only* 60 percent, why isn't it *more* than 60 percent? I have several jokes in my act that use true statistics: "Employers say they can't find good employees because (this is true) 72 percent of us lie on our resume." And then I ask myself questions like, "Why do we lie?" and "Who is lying?" or "What would make us stop lying?" to come up with the punch line, "OK, we'll quit lying on our resumes when they quit lying on the job descriptions."

Look at Opposites.

You can approach anything from the reverse perspective. If I know a fact about one group, then what does that mean for another group? For example: Almost one fourth of U.S. workers use computers at work to find a different job. . . . Because the other three fourths are jamming up the fax and copier with their resumes.

A study by the organizers of the British International Motor Show found that 47 percent of us regularly talk to our cars. The other 53 percent haven't given up on trying to make conversation with our spouses . . . yet.

Or how about taking the opposite approach? If we all believe that a certain thing is bad, then you could approach it as if it is actually good. "Reports are in that identity fraud is dropping. That's bad news. Apparently no one has credit good enough to steal."

When you're trying to come up with a line, ask yourself, "What is the reverse of this?" and "Can I take the opposite point of view?"

Link Things to News Items or Products.

A great way to make something funny quick or to freshen up a speech so that it *looks* like you just wrote your material yesterday is to link it to something recent people will recognize. Start off with a joke based on a recent news item or even a popular commercial that everyone's familiar with and people will make the connection immediately. Keep a running mental list of the top five popular commercials, and you could make a connection between a commercial and one of your environmental elements. Many companies are now offering their own "stimulus packages" as kind of a joke. The first one was funny. The millionth one is getting old. So be wary that you're not doing the joke that everyone is doing!

NOTE

Popular news items and commercials will give you quick references that people can relate to. "I did a show for Geico, the insurance company. That didn't go so well. I was standing backstage waiting to go on and I squashed this lizard."

A play on products also works, you just probably can't get the joke on TV, but you can still use it for laughs. My Slim Fast joke is a good example: "They've got all those diet pills and diet products out there. I'm just waiting for someone to bottle up some water from Mexico. 'Here, drink *this*. It'll make you lose some weight.' Call it Run Fast!"

The down side of writing about topical items is that you can come up with some great material and it's old in a month or less. You can't keep talking about Britney Spears and Kevin Federline's three-month marriage! The *good* news is, if you hang onto those jokes, the subject will always come back up and you can insert new names. Britney Spears may fade away, but you can guarantee some other young star will take her place at the bar, and bam! You've got fresh material.

RESEARCH TIPS FOR FAST FUNNY

*Don't just stop with what's in your
brain or the environment. Do 15 minutes
of research to find the funny fast!*

There are tons of other things you can do to come up with material fast. If you want to do some quick research, here are some ideas about where to look for material.

Websites/Newsletters.

If I'm trying to find out about an organization, I check out the websites for the company, the industry and the competitors. I once did a show for a religious group and they had a 15-page code of conduct on their website. OK, now what do we associate with religion? God, Jesus, the Bible, Mary, Joseph, the 10 commandments. Ahhh. . . there's the irony! And there's the joke. . . "I saw on your website that you had a 15-page code of conduct. I know you're faith-based and everything, but the Bible only has 10 commandments!" It got a huge laugh because even they saw that they were going a little overboard.

NOTE

When I hit a website, I don't spend a ton of time learning about the company. I go straight for the pages such as "history," "facts," "about" and maybe the latest press release. I can do more research if I want, but if I'm just trying to find the funny fast, those places will give me the best and quickest details.

High-Profile People.

I *do not* make fun of people, but I like to know about people who are high profile, and who don't mind a little kidding, as long as it's nice. If you can reference some common knowledge that most of the group has about someone, you can have some fun. Here are a couple of tips for when you're goofing around with people:

Make sure you get some detailed information about the person. "Bob likes to golf" isn't very descriptive and doesn't lead to many jokes. "Bob has a handicap of 50 and travels the world to play golf in every city" gives me a little more to work with. Also, remember that the majority of people must know about Bob's passion for golf. Otherwise, you'll hear a few laughs and see a lot of stares.

And most important, pick individuals who don't mind being in the limelight. Most people who are high profile with the company or organization don't mind a little kidding and actually like being mentioned. I finished a show one night for the dry bean industry where I'd had some fun with the VPs of Bush Beans and their golden retriever, Duke. As I was crossing the parking lot, a big stretch limo pulled up and the tinted windows rolled down. Inside was one of the VPs. I

NOTE

Finding out about people in the group has led me to some great lines:

I had fun with a guy who was getting ribbed by his coworkers for buying a Porsche. "Hey, Joe, congratulations on the new car. But we're confused. Everyone here in the room wants to know: When you buy one of those cars, is it pronounced Porsh-a . . . or middle-age crisis?"

And I once joked about a very tall man in the group who was known to drive a tiny sports car. "I'm the entertainment. It could be worse. We could all go out and just watch Bill get in and out of his sports car."

said, "I hope you enjoyed the show." He replied, "Thanks for mentioning us! That dog has made us a lot of money!" A word of caution when joking about people: Unless it's a celebrity, you shouldn't make fun of things like hair or makeup or, especially, weight. I've had groups say, "Oh, go ahead and have fun with her big hairdo." But I'm guessing she likes her big hairdo, so I stay away.

If you're not physically at an event, you can still have fun by making analogies between high profile people in the news, including celebrities, politicians and people who have done idiotic/weird things that we all remember. Just make sure you know your audience. The woman who had in vitro fertilization and delivered eight babies in addition to the six she already had may be funny to *you*, but in a business setting, there may be people in the audience who are on her side.

Competitors.

Yes, you can poke some fun at competitors. I wouldn't do it in a sales letter to customers, but I would at a sales rally where you're trying to pump up the troops. Not mean-spirited fun, but just some light humor is OK. I've done shows for credit unions that are having their convention in nice hotels, where I've poked fun at the banking convention being down the street in a (insert name of cheaper hotel) or, conversely, at the banking convention in the nicer hotel, I've made the same crack about the credit unions. So make your lists. What do you know about the competitor? What are the differences between this group and the competitors?

Again, don't do it to slam them hard . . . just light poking. I once heard some disc jockeys slamming the new radio station in town by, of all things, making fun of the new station's listeners! I was offended because I listened to both stations. And apparently many others were, too. The entire

> ## NOTE
>
> *Having fun with the competitor is OK, as long as it's not too mean. I did a show for John Deere, the tractor people. "That's a great name for a company—Deer—sleek, fast, runs like a deer. What were the guys over at Caterpillar thinking?" (Hey, if Caterpillar hires me, I'll have some fun with John Deere!)*

on-air and programming staff from the offending station was replaced within two weeks.

Awards.

Industry awards are always fun to play with as well; you can make up funny ones, put together fake requirements for winning or play off the names of the awards. Ask yourself questions like, "Why did this person win?" "What would you need to do to win?" "Who is winning?" Maybe the winner has an easy-to–pronounce name. "She met the major requirement for winning: We can pronounce her name!"

I was once performing comedy after an awards program in which they gave out 292 service awards for five years, 10 years, on up to 50 years of service at the hospital. Needless to say it was *late* when I got on stage, which gave me the perfect opening line: "It's nice to finally be on stage. I earned my five-year pin just sitting here."

Themes and Slogans.

Does the company or the event have a theme or slogan that you can have fun with? Themes and slogans are great to goof on because you can give other suggestions to replace them. You can also come up with a list of things that were considered but rejected, or even a list of how they came up with a slogan. For example, what are some other possible lines for the theme: "If you think you can, you're half way there"? How about . . .

- If you think you can, you've had way too much scotch!
- If you think you *can't*, you're probably right!
- If you think you can, you're half way *wrong*!

You also can pose theories about *why* a theme is being used. "We call this conference the 'learning forum' because no one's boss would allow them to come if we called it the 'drinking and golfing convention.'"

NOTE

Look at each word in a theme or slogan and see if there's something you can change to make the theme take on a different twist.

Stuff About the Audience/Industry Business Challenges/Industry Color/Gossip.

Does anything jump out at you that you hadn't thought about? Has anything big happened in the industry that you can play off of? Has there been a big scandal? Did a major firm go bankrupt?

I did a show for mushroom growers in Vegas, and the ceiling almost caved in from the laughter when I had a line about one of their biggest competitors who had just gone belly up after buying a bunch of mushroom farms. Everyone was happy they were gone because it was more money for them. I made a list of stereotypes about Vegas—gambling, losing lots of money, staying up late. And what was happening in their environment? A big mushroom grower went out of business. My line? "So I was watching people gamble last night, and I was talking to a dealer. He told me the only way you can lose money faster than at the craps table was by buying up mushroom farms." If you grow mushrooms, trust me, you'd be cracking up right now. But remember, I had permission from the organizers to make this crack.

10

CRAFTING THE HUMOR
SO IT FLOWS

*The Anatomy of a Joke: Jokes involve a setup
with the subject and facts and then a punch line
that highlights the irony, twists the joke in
another direction or gives an outrageous result.
Simple enough! But how do you structure it? Read on!*

OK, so I've talked about ways to put humor in communications fast:

- Get in the audience's mind and say what their sarcastic voice is thinking.
- Make connections between elements in the environment and stereotypes about those elements.
- Pull out the ironies and inconsistencies.
- Practice self-deprecation.
- Use joke formulas.
- Write callbacks and tags.
- Make twists with adages, acronyms, statistics, opposites, news items and familiar products.
- Research background information, prominent people, competitors, slogans and gossip.

I've also emphasized the importance of making lists and asking questions. I write fast and funny by doing all these things. Now for a bit on structure and a few other things you should pay attention to when writing humor. Hey, you might have a great irony, such as seeing smokers at a healthcare conference, but if you don't structure the joke correctly, it may not hit, or, at least, not as well as it could. Then you'll be back to square one thinking that you can't do comedy and my book didn't help. And really, I want to help. I want this book to be useful.

There are tons of ways to structure jokes. Here are a dozen quick lessons to get you going.

Recognize the Phenomenon of Three.

Three seems to be the magic number in comedy. If you're doing a joke where the punch line has a list, then make it three. The first two should be kind of factual and the third one is the twisted punch.

"My parents liked having four kids. But we're all grown up and out of the house. They actually got that 'empty nest syndrome,' so they replaced us with cats. Yeah, with cats my parents have found what they always wanted with kids—they clean themselves (factual), they don't talk back (kind of factual) and in a fit of anger, they *will* survive a drop from a second story window (twisted punch. . .what you sometimes *feel* like doing).

Maybe it's simply the fact that three puts people into a rhythm to laugh, which brings me to my next point.

NOTE

The power of three is important! According to a recent survey, 59 percent of doctors think that hospitals should:

> *A.) switch to a national health care plan*
> *B.) not accept Medicaid*
> *C.) be closer to golf courses*

Practice Cadence and Rhythm.

A lot of good jokes seem to have a beat that almost cues the audience when to laugh. This is a way to squeak by with a joke that might not be as funny as you'd like, but it's the rhythm that gets people. Most of my jokes are three lines long. Not sentences, but lines, when I type them out on the computer. OK, the one above is a little longer because of that whole three thing, but if it's straight setup and punch, try to keep it to three lines. And say it out loud. Sometimes you can just get a feel for the cadence and know if you need to add or delete a word by the way you say it.

Don't Repeat the Same Word.

If your setup and punch line both need to use the same word, don't use the *exact* same word. For example, if you're talking about a kid, use child, kid, the kid's name, whatever, so you don't keep saying kid. Of course, this rule can be broken, but in general, it's good advice.

Make Sure the Setup Is Clear.

Now here's an exception about repetition! If you have a somewhat complicated setup line, then say it twice, but in two different ways if possible *before* you say the punch.

For example:

"At my last job, my boss was into all of those team-building, TQM things. She kept telling me, 'Jan, you have to think outside the box, think outside the box.' . . . So I left my cubicle! TAG: I went to the bar. Now I *drink* outside the box."

Even though I don't change the words, I repeat the "think outside the box" phrase because I really want them to "get it" before I move on.

Also, take a look at your joke and underline the key words that the audience has to hear in order to "get it." Then make sure you're emphasizing that word or words.

You should also take the setup in steps and avoid giving too much information. That way people really understand it.

For example:

Setup: "I went to my class reunion. I was on the committee.
I was in charge of the invitations."

Punch line: "So there weren't any cheerleaders there
this year."

If I had put all of that setup into one sentence, "I was on my class reunion committee in charge of the invitations," it would have been information overload. The audience can't process the setup fast enough to hear the punch line. They'd be stuck back somewhere about me and my class reunion.

Don't Use Big Words.

People are not dumb. *But* the smaller the word you use, the less people have to think about it and process it to get the joke. A word like "ecstatic" will take an extra beat for them to catch up, and could easily be replaced by "thrilled." Short words make the recognition faster. This is imperative for *speaking* humor, not so much for writing it, except that you want the cadence to work.

Put the Punch at the End.

Of course, this is obvious, but you'd be surprised by how many speakers, writers and new comedians say or write the word that *should be* the punch line and then add a prepositional phrase after it. So make sure you're not doing that.

"A new study has found that the anti-anxiety drug fluvoxamine (so much for short words) is effective in relieving anxiety in school-age children. Of course, it's not quite as effective as getting their braces off."

The words "their teeth" don't need to be at the end because we already get it and it would just slow down the joke.

"The first bloodless surgery was performed this week. A kid who is a Jehovah's Witness got a new liver without a blood transfusion. The parents were so happy, they *almost* celebrated!" The word "celebrated" is the punch. No need to say "celebrated his survival."

Of course sometimes it's hard to know where the punch is, and I've even had the audience laugh at a place in the setup that made me realize where the punch line really is. My joke about a show for a women's group is a good example of this. "I did a show for a women's group. In the morning they had a program on how to stop trying to change your man, and in the afternoon they had a shooting clinic." I didn't realize that last line was the punch, so I was going to go on with something like "and everyone attended" or "the clinic was packed." It was only after the audience laughed at that point and, luckily, I took a breath long enough to hear it, I realized that *that's* where the joke lay. The fact that there was a shooting clinic was ironic enough. It wasn't important to say there was huge attendance.

So check your punch line and make sure that the last word, or pretty close to the last word, is the funny word. The twist. The connection. The surprise. The thing that will make 'em laugh. No prepositional phrases or other words after that word. Really. I'm not kidding.

Twist Words for the Joke.

When I follow speakers and I'm looking for an opening line, I listen to what they're saying to try and find the *one or a few words* that I can twist or have fun with. I mentioned the kids singing in the casino earlier. I heard the other speaker say that it was "wholesome." Realizing the environment was anything but gave me the word that I could key in on to have some fun. And with the "glitz and glamour" story, those words kept coming up, so I used those to twist it. Many speakers are so focused on what they have to say that they don't focus on what is happening ahead of them. You should know your opening lines so well that you have the freedom to pay attention to your environment. Listen closely for key words that you can twist or take literally or apply to yourself. These will give you a great opening joke.

Use the "Cuh" Sound.

A general comedy rule is that words with the "c" or "k" sound are funny. Who knows if this is true, but you have to admit, the names Chuck and Cletus are funnier than Steve and Stuart. So if you can substitute a K or C word in place of another word, do it.

Make the Connection in Their Heads.

The whole thing with a joke is to say something without saying it. It's much funnier to have people make a connection in their heads than if you spell it out. This allows you to say something a little dicey (without being dirty) that we all "get" in our heads. "I once used my mom's birth control pills in my science fair project. This is true; the estrogen in the pills makes plants grow. I won the science fair . . . and got a new baby sister!" We all get it, it's funny and cute and there was no need to get graphic.

Exaggerate—Take Things to the Extreme.

Exaggerate, exaggerate, exaggerate! Comedy is about exaggeration. Don't say somebody is 100 years old; say they're a thousand years old. That's just funnier because there's *no way* they could be a thousand years old. Even 100-year-old people will laugh at that. Exaggerate the punch line; *don't exaggerate the setup.* I talk about my family vacations growing up and how my dad smoked three packs a day in the car with the windows rolled up. To make sure everyone knew how much he smoked and how bad that was, I tried saying he smoked 10 packs a day. But saying that in the setup didn't work because people were hung up on someone who smoked that much. Three packs seemed to be a believable, but huge, amount someone might smoke.

Be Brief.

Bill Cosby may be the only person who can go on and on and on. The rest of us should wrap it up quickly. Remember, if you're going to rattle away, you better have a *REALLY, REALLY* good punch line at the end. So be as brief as you can. Use my three-line standard if you can. Put in just what you need and stop.

Be Specific.

The more specific you are, the funnier the joke will be. If you're talking about fast food for example, don't just say fast food, go ahead and name a restaurant. If you're talking about a number, don't pick 100 or 200. Use a number that's really specific like 132 or 249. This makes the joke sound more real, which can make it more absurd.

NOTE

Don't think of it as a joke, think of it as a conversation. You know where you're going with it and you know the essence of the punch line, so relax and let your words come out naturally. You'll surprise yourself. Thinking of a joke as a conversation will also take the pressure off trying to make a line work, which helps ensure it will work.

11

CHAPTER

RULES OF HUMOR

The allure of comedy clubs is that we get to watch comedians "break all the rules" with their uninhibited humor. The reality is most of us should pay attention to some (unspoken) rules.

Comedy has few rules, which is what makes it fun. But if you're going to add humor to your communications, there are a few things you can pay attention to so you don't get in trouble.

Be a Part of the Club.

In general, only make fun of groups that you are a member of. We women can have a lot of fun with women. Guys can't make so much fun of women. They do in the comedy clubs, but overall, guys have to be careful making fun of women. Perhaps they can talk about their wives, but they'd better not be too harsh.

Now, on the reverse side, sometimes women can make more fun of guys because guys are supposed to be able to take it. But really, ladies, that's why we've got the bad rep with men for man-bashing. So be a little more creative when being funny and leave the men alone.

And actually, a big rule is to leave women alone, period. Even in comedy clubs, the woman has to be really, really obnoxious and the audience has to be really, really tired of her before you can even poke gentle fun.

So if you're a member of the club, make sure everyone knows you're a member before you start poking fun. I'm tall, people see that I'm tall, so I can make fun of being tall. Comics can bend this rule a bit because when we go on stage, people know we're there to make jokes. But if you're giving a speech and you're *not* a comic, then don't bend this club rule.

Be True to Yourself.

People can see through insincerity. So do humor that you truly think is funny, and you'll sell it. If you do humor that you think *might* be funny and you're hoping to slide by for a laugh, you probably won't. Most comics talk about what

> **NOTE**
>
> *I have big feet, so I can make fun of people with big feet after I've told people I have big feet. If people didn't know I wear a size 12-AAA shoe, then I'd just look like a jerk for making jokes about anyone with big feet.*

bugs them in the world, whether it's politics, the educational system or their relationships. I talk a lot about work, which is why I go by The Work Lady.® Many of the wacky rules and crazy policies at the office bother me, and that's what I enjoy making fun of.

Understand Different Cultures.

Americans have been taught to "start your speech off with a joke," but other cultures may not do this. And even if you're speaking in the U.S., there are non-Americans in your audience who may not appreciate the humor. I once performed for 800 people and 799 were cracking up about my jokes on the company, while the Italian CEO glared at me. He was fine later when someone explained it to him, but, a few jokes in, I dropped what I'd written on the company and just did my standard show. Unfortunately, they missed out because he didn't get the memo.

Keep it Clean.

I would usually say, don't swear or tell off-color jokes, *ever*. But I really don't know what your purpose is for adding humor, so I can't make that statement. I *can* say that for business purposes, you should not get "dirty." I've done shows for every type of group, and I've had people say, *"Oh, you can get a little edgy."* My response is, "No, thanks. I'd rather keep working." My feeling is that even if I'm in front a group that cusses every other word, there is probably still someone in the room who is offended—whether they speak up or not. So err on the side of caution. I can defend myself if I bomb using clean humor (bad match with the group perhaps), but if I rock the room using blue humor, and just one person complains, I can't really defend why I used it. A good rule of thumb is, if you're not sure if the joke is clean enough, *don't do it.* I once did a show for some contractors in which I bombed badly. Afterwards the president said, "These are contractors, you should've done d__ (below the belt) jokes." Ironically, I was following a speaker who talked about how some contractors need to change their unprofessional image. Go figure.

NOTE

Think Funny—Read Other Stuff.

There's lots of funny out in the world. Read it! If you're looking for some news items to kick off topical material, read USA Today. *The way it's written, the setup lines are almost done for you. And read tabloids. Yes, I said read tabloids! (privately, when no one is looking) Their writers know how to write outrageous articles and you might just learn a thing or two about being outrageous in your punch lines. A guy I know owns an engineering firm, and he used to make all his employees who were going to do any kind of writing read* The Weekly World News *because it was wacky and would get them thinking creatively. That paper has since gone out of publication, but I'm guessing he still makes them read something to keep their minds thinking differently.*

NOTE

Edgy or Inappropriate — Walking a Thin Line
A lot of people, including many new comics, call themselves "edgy" when in reality their stuff is just dirty. (My apologies to my comic friends who really are edgy and funny!) You don't have to be dirty to be funny. That said, you have to be true to yourself and do the humor that works for you. If you cuss every other word, and that's how you express yourself, then find venues for your humor that accept that style. The comics who rise to the top aren't the ones who are the cleanest or the dirtiest. They're the ones who do humor that reflects their own views and the way they see life.

Don't Steal.

Period. This book is about writing *your own* humor, not "borrowing" from others. If you heard a great line at an event, and even though the chances are a gazillion to zero that people will know you took it, don't. Someone has spent time being original and you don't have the right to take that line; karma will catch up to you. Of course, you can always ask for permission, but if it's not granted, leave the line alone.

12

MEMORY TECHNIQUES

I kick off most of my corporate and association shows with 20 or more new jokes on the group. I don't spend weeks practicing them, I just use a few techniques.

If you're giving a speech or trying to start off a meeting or even doing some one-on-one networking, and you have the perfect line to kick it off, the challenge is to *remember* the darn thing. I do 20 or more new jokes for each event, 99 percent of which I won't do again unless I'm in a similar industry, so I've got to remember a lot of stuff. Practice goes without saying, so I won't advise you to do that. (You *must* do that!) Here's what I do to help my memory:

Sleep on It.

I go over my jokes right before I go to bed at night. There really *is* a connection between sleeping and memory. A friend of mine was actually doing research on it at a university. But what I can tell you from my own experience is that saying the lines right before I go to bed really helps me remember them the next day. Try it!

Say it Fast.

In preparation for a show, I say all of my jokes, new and old, as fast as I can out loud. This kind of ingrains the jokes in my brain so that when I say them on stage, slower, they roll out conversationally. Try it yourself. Take a few jokes or a paragraph of something you want to remember, and run through it at breakneck speed a couple times out loud. In your head doesn't count. You'll be amazed at how relaxed it comes out sounding when you're under the gun to say it.

Rely on One-Word Reminders.

I bring a list to the stage with me that has one-word reminders, like train or airplane or whatever the joke involves. These words cue me so I know what joke is next. Comics and musicians call these one-word reminders "set lists," and they are basically the order of the show. A lot of times, the word I write on my set list is the word I'm having trouble remembering. I could write "doctors" if the joke is about doctors performing a heart bypass. But if I'm having trouble remembering "bypass," then I use that word instead.

Since I don't work behind a podium, I usually have to acknowledge to the audience the paper in my hand, so I'll start out with something like, "I took some notes on you guys today." That way people aren't wondering what's in my hand. And even if I think I know the jokes cold backward and forward, I still bring the set list with me in my pocket. I remember the night I went blank in front of 500 mushroom growers and had no notes on stage. Luckily, after about 30 seconds I remembered a killer line to get things rolling, but never again will I go up "unarmed." It was a long 30 seconds!

Group Things Together.

I make categories for my jokes, like "the room," "the event," "the people," "the food." Then I put all my one-word reminders under the category they relate to. This not only aids my memory, but also keeps me organized so I'm not all over the place with the jokes.

Know Your First Joke Cold.

Your first joke is your most important one because if it hits, you build confidence. If it dies, you will be hesitant to try any others. So make sure you know that one really well.

Start with Your Newest Jokes.

Public speaking wisdom says to start with a joke to relax your audience. I say start with jokes you've just developed on the fly because it's easier to remember them. If you wrote something while sitting at a conference, and then you bury it in your speech, chances are you won't remember the wording when you get to it; reading your one-word reminder, such as "car," will just draw a blank.

CHAPTER 13

BOMBING, DYING AND KILLING—
HUMOR IS SUBJECTIVE.

Sadly, sometimes your best lines are funny only to you.

Appropriately, "unlucky" chapter 13 addresses bombing, dying and killing. These are the three adjectives comics use to describe how good or bad their show went. Bombing and dying are not good. Killing is wonderful! I think the fear of bombing is what keeps most people from even trying humor. Sure, not getting a laugh stinks, but you have to remember that humor is subjective. Not everyone is going to get it or think like you. The majority probably will get it, and *that* pay off is wonderful. By the way, any comic who says he hasn't bombed is *lying*. Having a joke go flat is part of the process, and you will not hit a home run every time.

"I have a friend who just had a liver transplant, and he went to his liver transplant support group picnic, you know, where you bring somebody *else's* side dish."

Not everybody likes that joke. In fact, I get a lot of groans from it. But I *like* that joke, it's funny to me, and it's true. Plus my friend with the transplant is OK, so I have license to laugh about it. Every couple of shows I throw out that joke just to get a reaction and to have some fun with it. I'll always think it's a good joke, but humor is subjective. So don't worry about whether someone is going to like your humor or not. Just have fun with what you think is funny.

The joke I open with in my current act actually got dead silence the first time I used it. I waited six months before I did it again but I kept thinking, *"This is funny. This is funny,"* so I tried it one more time and it hit *big*. Maybe the first time it was the audience or the way I said it. But I'm glad I tried it again. So don't discount the humor the first time you try a new joke. Here are a few tips for when you have a joke go flat:

Have a Saver Line.

If I'm doing a show for an accounting group, for example, and one of the custom jokes I wrote for them doesn't hit, then

I just toss out a saver line, such as, "Hey, cut me a break, I'm just trying to make accounting funny." That usually gets a laugh and a little appreciation that I'm *trying*. Come up with a few saver lines of your own to toss out.

Move On.

Some comics say that you should *never* mention a joke that bombs. I'd say don't keep mentioning it. Mention it once if you feel you have to and then move on. If you've had a couple of lines that didn't work, don't keep pointing them out or the group will start keeping score. And, for gosh sakes, let it go immediately. If you keep it in the back of your head, I guarantee it'll affect your entire presentation. I still have flashbacks about bombing in front of 200 coal miners my second year into comedy. The first 60 seconds, I fast-forwarded through my entire act and thought, "They are going to hate everything." And I was right! It was a long, torturous show.

NOTE

"Hey, is this mike on?" is a popular saver line for new comics. Don't use it! It marks you as a newbie just learning how to use a mike.

Don't focus on what you don't want to happen.

Focus on selling the joke and having fun with it. If your mantra is "I hope this doesn't bomb," then it probably will.

Remember, It Might Not Be the Joke.

Sure, you could've said the joke wrong or maybe it really wasn't funny. But you have to realize that many times it may not be the joke. Maybe that's the way this group *always* responds to humor or maybe they're in a bad mood or maybe half of them just got laid off. Don't give up on what you think is a good joke. Re-think it. See if it needs to be restructured. Then try telling it to another audience to test its worthiness.

THANKS! THAT'S MY TIME...

That's the line many comedians wrap up with! I'd like to add a little more. Thanks again for reading this book. I hope you've picked up more than a few tips to punch up your communications so you'll have more fun with the written and spoken word and your audiences will, too.

The key to much of this is doing it—a lot! You won't get good at coming up with fast funny if you try it just once or twice. Get in the habit of looking for the funny when there is no pressure, like when you're dealing with customer service people, and then it'll come more naturally when you're under the gun to add some funny.

And don't get overwhelmed by trying to do all these things. Just pick one or two techniques that resonate with you and try them out. Then at your next high school reunion people will wonder why they didn't vote *you* as class clown.

Jan
Jan@TheWorkLady.com
www.The WorkLady.com

ABOUT THE AUTHOR

When she was 10 years old, Jan declared to her parents that once she turned 16, she was going to "buy a motorcycle, ride cross-country to Los Angeles and become a comedian." Her parents didn't quite share her "vision" so she ended up graduating from Virginia Tech and having a marketing career for over a decade before getting on stage. Today, 16 years into her comedy career, Jan has performed for thousands of groups, and she's been featured in *The Wall Street Journal* as a top convention comedian whose act is clean. Jan has also sold comedy material to just about everyone on the planet—from late night TV shows, to hundreds of radio stations, CEOs and professional speakers. And yes, Jan did finally make it cross-country to Los Angeles, where she currently resides, *and* she just bought a motor scooter!

NOTE

For more information about booking Jan for a speaking engagement or using her talents to help bring humor to your communications, contact her at www.TheWorkLady.com or Jan@TheWorkLady.com

9 780984 099900